MODERN HERALDRY: VOLUME 2

A new selection of trademarks and symbols from around the globe, based on heraldic imagery, makes up the second volume of this well-received graphic design publication.

As part of Counter-Print's wide survey of logo design, the starting point for this series was the observation that many present day marks still draw upon traditional symbols such as the heraldic mark or logos that share its characteristics.

In volume one we were particularly interested in exploring, visually, the juxtaposition between a historic art form and its modern interpretation and this book is a continuation of this visual documentation.

Five years on from the first volume, the popularity of heraldry, it seems, has not diminished. Audiences perhaps respond well to nostalgia, with many designers keen to capture the visual romance and history of a brand or convey craftsmanship. Present day companies still often use heraldry as a means of corporate identity. From banks, train lines, schools and churches to universities, football clubs and societies – heraldry is still a potent modern symbol.

However, the heraldic mark now very rarely derives from the founder's family crest and is much more commonly used to convey a sense of respectability or authenticity for a commercial venture.

Historically, a coat of arms was a unique heraldic design on a shield, used by medieval knights to identify the wearer. A knight's battle armour was prestigious and conveyed his achievements, so the coat of arms evolved into a status symbol that provided insight into family history, property, profession or occupation.

Heraldry, in it's simplest form, was a method of visual communication, creating an instant message, both to the highly informed and the illiterate. In ancient times, a banner had to be simple enough to be read by a man on a galloping horse and the outcome of misreading such symbology could cost him his life.

There were many imaginative variations and combinations in every crest design that identified the particular carrier or owner of that crest. Each symbol was chosen for it's meaning. Flowers had connotations surrounding hope and joy, while fruit signified bounty and peace. Animals were frequently used, usually in positions of combat, and the animals chosen were ferocious-looking or represented positive traits such as wisdom, resourcefulness and loyalty.

Modern heraldry, as documented within this book, can be seen as an extension of this. Yes, it often denotes heritage or authenticity but it can also have multiple meanings invested in the choice of symbolism used.

Each element of a coat of arms can be subjective or literal. For example, sometimes the audience is asked to make visual leaps when elements are chosen to represent the geographical origins of a product or to read the marks literally when books are chosen for publishers, pens for copywriters and so on.

Traditionally, significant meaning would also be invested via colour used in heraldry. Gold denoting generosity, silver for peace and red suggesting military strength for example. As such, our decision to reproduce the logos in black and white might seem strange but it is a decision based on our belief that all logos should work as well in monochrome as in full colour. The modern logo, in contrast to historic heraldry, has a myriad of functions that require it to be legible in colour and in black and white, often down to the size of a favicon or social media icon.

Despite our modern obsession with technology, there has been a leaning towards craftsmanship and quality in what we choose to consume, in opposition to mass production and globalisation, and the style of the logos collected in this book reflect this trend.

This could be termed as a kind of 'neo-nostalgia' which many designers turn to, creating modern marks that share historic, often heraldic, visual cues in order to convey a sense of respectability, dignity and dependability for their client.

This traditional aesthetic arguably resonates so strongly among designers because it reflects the history behind brand-making. This can be seen both stylistically – before computers it was all handmade – and in it's construction, with the laurel, shield, seal, crest etc, chosen to display information.

Today's designers are lucky enough to be equipped, thanks to the web, with an encyclopedic grasp of design history and are able to use historical reference as inspiration. They are designing marks that intentionally counteract the highly-polished, digital-based logos associated with mass-consumerism; turning instead to craft-based mediums such as hand lettering, stamps, traditional symbolism and historic embellishment. The combination of the old and the new, craftsmanship and technology, often creates a fertile breeding ground for innovative logo solutions and marks that are invested with layered meaning as well as beautiful aesthetics.

The logo designs within this book are grouped under category headings chosen for their heraldic connotations. The categories included are: shields, crests, stamps, seals, laurels, flags and crowns as these were the main devices we identified as being popular in contemporary heraldic designs.

Jon Dowling
Counter-Print

SHIELDS

1

2

3

4

5

1. Rathfinny Wine Estate
English sparkling wine
United Kingdom
Aloof/Pentagram
aloof.co
pentagram.com
2015

2. Zenith
Finance broker
United Kingdom
Alan Cheetham
behance.net/booyah
2018

3. MPLS Parks
Non-profit fundraiser
to protect city parks
USA
Leslie Olson
leslielynneolson.com
2017

4. Nizam Bashir Law
Law firm
USA
Yossi Belkin Design Co.
yossibelkin.com
2015

5. Geoff Cox
Automotive
United Kingdom
Alt Design
alt-design.net
2018

6. Stockholm Stad
Public service
Sweden
Essen International
esseninternational.com
2012

7. The Minster School
Independent school
United Kingdom
Fettle
fettledesign.com
2016

6

7

8. Rooster Republic
Publishing
Croatia
Type08
type08.com
2018

9. Roostiq
Bars & restaurants
USA
Type08
type08.com
2019

8

ROOSTIQ
GRILL BAR ~ POULTRY LIKE A POETRY

10. Concours Hippiques
Blog about horse shows
France
Atelier Atlantique
atelieratlantique.fr
2008

11. Urban Contours
Land surveyors
United Kingdom
Alt Design
alt-design.net
2018

10

11

12. Nikolov & Partners
Law firm
Bulgaria
BRVND
brvnd.com
2017

13. The Brooklyn Castle
Commercial real estate
USA
Krinsky Design
krinskydesign.com
2018

12

13

14. Nemo Equipment
Outdoor equipment
USA
HAM
madebyham.com
2018

15. Small Giants
Creative/ad agency
USA
Rinker Design Co.
rinker.co
2012

16. Axcent
Financial services
Mexico
Saturna Studio
saturnastudio.com
2017

14

15

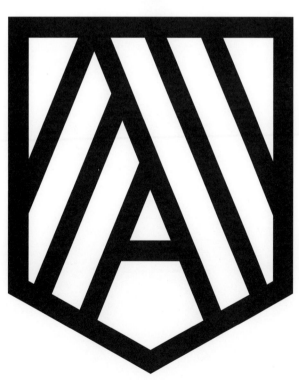

16

17

18

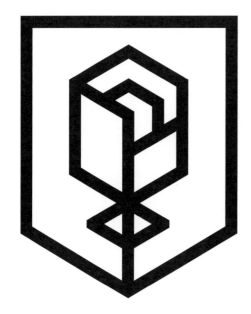

19

20

21

17. Corporate Fashion
Fashion
Germany
Hochburg Design Studio
hochburg.design
2013

18. Clover House
Real estate property
USA
Krinsky Design
krinskydesign.com
2019

19. Rose House Detroit
Real estate
USA
Type08
type08.com
2017

20. Brown & Vautier
Law firm
United Kingdom
Ascend Studio
ascendstudio.co.uk
2018

21. Keystone Barbers
Barbershop & male grooming
products
United Kingdom
Aidan Croucher
behance.net/aidancroucher
2019

22. Maria Rigol Ordi
Wine celler
Spain
Atipus
atipus.com
2015

23. Sunday Suns
Self-initiated
USA
Carpenter Collective
carpentercollective.com
2018

22

23

24. Albdoc
Cosmetics
Germany
Hochburg Design Studio
hochburg.design
2015

25. The Ivy School
Education
Pakistan
Type08
type08.com
2018

26

27   28

29. Arzberger Stationers
Speciality custom
printer/stationer
USA
SDCO Partners
sdcopartners.com
2017

30. Hausmann
Wine glasses
Brazil
Pedro Paulino
pedropaulino.com
2017

31. Huyze De Baere
Restaurant
Belgium
Chilli
chilli.be
2016

32. Figaro
Bar & restaurant
Japan
COMMUNE
commune-inc.jp
2015

33. USA Soccer
Self-initiated
USA
Rinker Design Co.
rinker.co
2014

29   30

31   32

33

34. Bird Clan
Publishing
Croatia
Type08
type08.com
2018

35. Alfie & Co.
Coffee roaster
United Kingdom
Cause & Effect
causeandeffect.design
2016

34

35

37. Veugelaers Investment
Real estate projects
Belgium
Chilli
chilli.be
2017

**36. Family Waldruche
de Montremy**
Family estate
France
FL@33, Agathe Jacquillat
& Tomi Vollauschek
flat33.com
2019

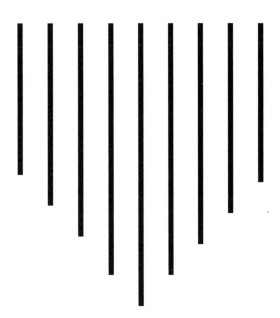

36

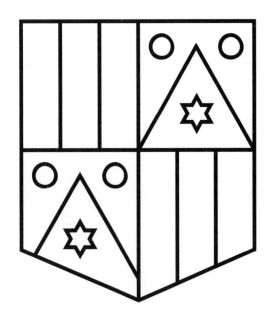

37

38

39

40

41

43

44

38. HCC
Talent acquisition
Poland
Dmowski & Co.
dmowski.co
2015

**39. Boulder Mountain
Crossfit**
Gym
USA
Rinker Design Co.
rinker.co
2015

40. City of Helsinki
City
Finland
Werklig
werklig.com
2018

41. Uris Pride
Lawyers
Russia
Apus
apus.agency
2015

42. L. M. Stern
Real estate investment
Ascend Studio
ascendstudio.co.uk
2018

43. Kuvalis
Private children's school
USA
Austin McKinney
axmckinney.com
2019

44. FIA
Arts school
USA
Yossi Belkin Design Co.
yossibelkin.com
2017

**45. The Happy Living
Project**
Environmental consultant
New Zealand
makebardo
makebardo.com
2018

**46. Native Sons of
the Mountain West**
Collective
USA
Rinker Design Co.
rinker.co
2015

45

46

47. The Football Crest Index
Documenting football crests from around
the world
United Kingdom
Studio Beuro
studiobeuro.co.uk
2016

48. Juventus
Sport entertainment company whose
core asset is the leading Italian
professional football team
Italy
Interbrand
interbrand.com
2017

49. Crossfit Leeuwarden
Crossfit, high intensity
interval training
The Netherlands
Maxwell A. Davis/
Three Bears Theory
studiotbt.com
2015

50. Celler Masroig
Wine celler
Spain
Atipus
atipus.com
2016

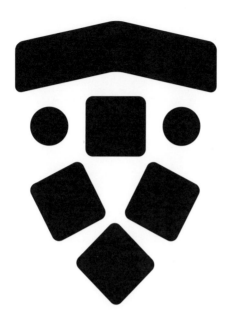

49

50

51. Wilkes School
Private education
USA
Ashton Design
ashton-design.com
2017

52. Perrier Jablonski
Consulting agency
France
BangBang Studio
bangbang.ca
2012

51

52

53. Grey Croft Inn
Hotel/hospitality
USA
SDCO Partners
sdcopartners.com
2016

SEALS

54. Blue Valley Dairy Farm
Dairy farm
USA
Yossi Belkin Design Co.
yossibelkin.com
2017

55. Hereford True Beef
Beef brand developed &
owned by Herefords Australia
Australia
End of Work
endofwork.com.au
2015

56. Farm & Fable
Retail store
USA
Ōyay
oyay.co
2013

57. Alden & Harlow
Restaurant
USA
Ōyay
oyay.co
2013

58. The Craft Room
Eatery
USA
Yossi Belkin Design Co.
yossibelkin.com
2017

54   55

56

57   58

59. Studio Ghezhi
Letterpress printer
Taiwan, China
Maxwell A. Davis/Three Bears Theory
studiotbt.com
2017

60. Grinning Face Gelato
Gelato
Canada
Leo Burnett Design
Leoburnettdesign.ca
2015

61. Robinson Webster
Independent retail
property advisor
United Kingdom
Interabang
interabang.uk
2016

62. Canelé du Japon doudou
Confectionery store
Japan
Zealplus
zealplus.co.jp
2014

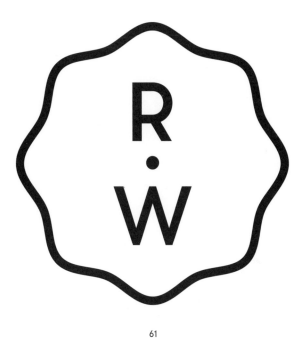

61

62

63

64

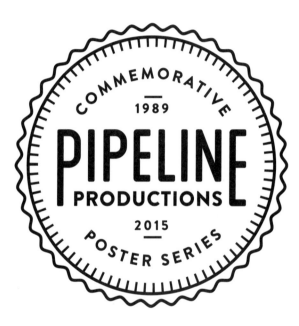

65

66

67

63. Sukitto
Specialty dry cleaning
Japan
COMMUNE
commune-inc.jp
2013

64. Yoli Tortilleria
Food
USA
Carpenter Collective
carpentercollective.com
2019

65. Pipeline Productions
Music
USA
Carpenter Collective
carpentercollective.com
2016

66. Woods River Cruises
River Thames boat company
United Kingdom
Peter Horridge
horridge.com
2013

67. Atlas
High-end lofts
USA
Carpenter Collective
carpentercollective.com
2017

EST 2010

68. Lumine Salon
Salon
USA
Carpenter Collective
carpentercollective.com
2015

69. Boehme's Batch
Candy/food service
USA
Carpenter Collective
carpentercollective.com
2017

70. Port Noonan Yacht Club
Apparel/goods
USA
Rinker Design Co.
Rinker.co
2010

69

70

CROWNS

71. Crown Ocean Capital
Venture capital firm
Monaco
BRVND
brvnd.com
2017

72. Regal Coffee
Coffee roasters
Poland
Dmowski & Co.
dmowski.co
2019

71

72

73. Monarch
Cosmetics brand
Bulgaria
BRVND
brvnd.com
2018

74. Tabassum
Jewellery
USA
Studio MPLS
studiompls.com
2016

73

74

75. Monticelle
Wine
Belgium
Chilli
chilli.be
2015

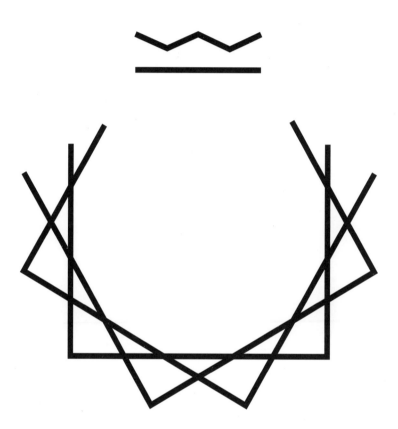

76. Lionhead
Builder
Canada
idApostle
idapostle.com
2016

77

78

79

80

81

77. Invest in Heads
Investment
Germany
Hochburg Design Studio
hochburg.design
2017

78. Cult Club
Private club for men
Russia
Apus
apus.agency
2014

79. Bulgari
Rakia brand
USA
BRVND
brvnd.com
2016

80. Good Queen Bess
Skincare/beauty
USA
SDCO Partners
sdcopartners.com
2016

81. Henry the Dentist
Dental industry
USA
Hinterland
hinterlandstudio.com
2019

82. Biji Coffee
Coffee maker
Russia
Apus
apus.agency
2015

83. Queens Pavilion
Commercial real estate
USA
Krinsky Design
krinskydesign.com
2018

82

83

EST 018

84. Meat Market Russia
Meat industry
Russia
Type08
type08.com
2018

85. Nacion
Real estate development project
Mexico
Anagrama
anagrama.com
2014

86. Scottish Police Federation
Services to the Police Force
United Kingdom
Cause & Effect
causeandeffect.design
2019

87. Solifer
Bicycle producer
Finland
Werklig
werklig.com
2017

88

89

90

91

88. Admiralty Arch
Property development
United Kingdom
Peter Horridge
horridge.com
2016

89. Cornwall Terrace
Luxury property
development
United Kingdom
Peter Horridge
horridge.com
2010

90. Duchess of York
Duchess
United Kingdom
Peter Horridge
horridge.com
2010

91. Maison de Bruges
Artisan confiture
Belgium
Chilli
chilli.be
2013

92. English Gins
Promotion of the English gins
Industry
France
Peter Horridge
horridge.com
2010

92

93. Marks & Spencer
Own brand Champagne
United Kingdom
Peter Horridge
horridge.com
2013

94. Get Em Tiger
Creative agency
USA
Jessica Benhar
harkenback.com.au
2019

93

94

95. Kingdom
Creative digital design agency
Poland
Mateusz Turbinski
turbinski.com
2014

96. KMCC Accounting
Accounting
Poland
Mateusz Turbinski
turbinski.com
2014

97. Circuito PRE
Horse farm/ranch
Mexico
Saturna Studio
saturnastudio.com
2017

98. Artidote
Handmade luxury candles
China
Jessica Benhar
harkenback.com.au
2017

97

98

99. Her Royal Honey
Candy product
USA
Yossi Belkin Design Co.
yossibelkin.com
2017

100. Salsas El Conde Nava
Hot sauce production
Mexico
Saturna Studio
saturnastudio.com
2015

101. Imperial Heat
High-quality wood fuel
products
New Zealand
BRVND
brvnd.com
2016

102. La Brea
Restaurant
USA
Yossi Belkin Design Co.
yossibelkin.com
2016

103. King Road Brewing Co
Brewery
Australia
Stuart Smythe
stuartsmythe.com
2015

99

100

101

102

103

104. Queen Made
Food company
Japan
Grand Deluxe
grand-deluxe.com
2018

105. El Rocko Lounge
Cocktail bar
USA
Kyle Poff
kylepoff.com
2016

104

105

STAMPS

106

107

106. Brav
Cabinet of curiosities
France
Atelier Atlantique
atelieratlantique.fr
2014

107. Green Orchard
Juice company
USA
Yossi Belkin Design Co.
yossibelkin.com
2015

108. Queenstown Life
Blog telling stories about
brands & business
New Zealand
makebardo
makebardo.com
2018

109. Carter's Coffee Co.
Coffee shop
USA
Aidan Croucher
behance.net/aidancroucher
2017

110. Middle of Nowhere
Homeware design
Australia
Mildred & Duck
mildredandduck.com
2011

108

109

110

**111. MAJORMAJOR
Design Co.**
Design & marketing
Germany
Hannes Beer
hannesbeer.de
2017

112. Olipop
Sparkling tonics
USA
Break Maiden
breakmaiden.co
2018

**113. Green Bench
Brewing Co.**
Brewery
USA
Break Maiden
breakmaiden.co
2019

111   112

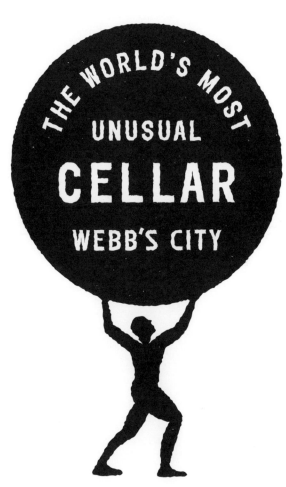

113

114. Maryland Distiller's Guild
Association
USA
Ashton Design
ashton-design.com
2015

115. Anatomy of a Fighter
Production company
USA
Brandon Nickerson
bnicks.com
2019

116   117

118

119   120

116. The Empanada Kitchen
Food
New Zealand
makebardo
makebardo.com
2017

117. Fillmore Wine Club
Association for
wine connoisseurs
USA
Brandon Nickerson
bnicks.com
2018

118. Korshags Food AB
Seafood suppliers
Swedan
Kurppa Hosk
kurppahosk.com
2017

119. Costa Rica Surf Realty
Real estate/travel
Costa Rica
Rinker Design Co.
rinker.co
2014

120. Whistling Hare Distillery
Distillery
USA
Cast Iron Design
castirondesign.com
2015

121. Seedlings
Restaurant
Canada
Doublenaut
doublenaut.com
2018

122. Imkerei Huschidarian
Beekeeper
Germany
Hannes Beer
hannesbeer.de
2016

123. Low Hanging Fruits
Group/musician
United Kingdom
Cause & Effect
causeandeffect.design
2018

124. Made Coffee
Coffee roasters
USA
Break Maiden
breakmaiden.co
2018

125. Chicago Sign Co.
Sign painting
USA
Break Maiden
breakmaiden.co
2018

121

122

123

124

125

126

127

128

129

130

126. Stirling Yachting
Yacht charters
United Kingdom
Ascend Studio
ascendstudio.co.uk
2018

127. Spin Toronto
Ping pong bar
Canada
Doublenaut
doublenaut.com
2015

128. Sapientia
Social club
Canada
Doublenaut
doublenaut.com
2017

129. Coal Miner's Daughter
Clothing
Canada
Doublenaut
doublenaut.com
2014

130. Tenzing
Skin care/grooming for men
United Kingdom
Mash Creative
mashcreative.co.uk
2015

131. Cascade Lodge
Hospitality
USA
Leslie Olson
leslielynneolson.com
2018

132. Chani Greenbaum
Event planning
USA
Krinsky Design
krinskydesign.com
2018

133. Shropshire Design
Furniture & interiors
United Kingdom
Alan Cheetham
behance.net/booyah
2015

134. Atelier 19
Jewellery store
France
Alexia Roux
alexiaroux.fr
2017

135. Wild Grace
Botanical skincare products
Canada
Studio July
studiojuly.co
2018

131

132

133

134

135

136. Dyrenes Beskyttelse
Denmark's leading animal welfare NGO
Denmark
Re-public
re-public.com
2017

137. Jacob Moe
Producer
Greece
Pedro Paulino
pedropaulino.com
2016

138

139

140

141

138. Manos de Cacao
Chocolate brand
Mexico
Anagrama
anagrama.com
2018

139. Keep Investing
Property developers
United Kingdom
Alan Cheetham
behance.net/booyah
2018

140. Asakara Good Store
Café
Japan
otto design lab.
8otto.com
2018

141. Maison Lem
Culinary supply & education
USA
Parker
designbyparker.com
2016

142. Kitz
Hotel
Germany
Hochburg Design Studio
hochburg.design
2018

142

143. Yonder
Hospitality
New Zealand
makebardo
makebardo.com
2017

144. Dig Inn
Fast casual food concept
USA
High Tide
hightidenyc.com
2017

145. Cibic & Hanke
Business strategy
Germany
Hochburg Design Studio
hochburg.design
2014

146. The Bakeshop
Cupcake café & shop
Japan
COMMUNE
commune-inc.jp
2018

147. Stereohype
Graphic art label
& online boutique
Austria
FL@33, Tomi Vollauschek
& Agathe Jacquillat
flat33.com

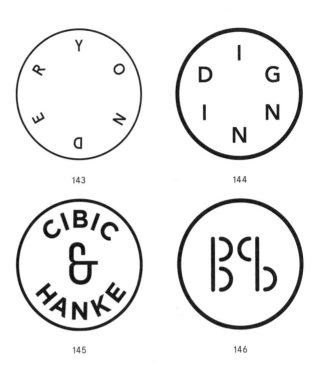

143   144

145   146

147

148. Las Rozas
A salon to celebrate
weddings
Spain
Maria Design
maria–design.es
2017

149. Jardin des Sens
Restaurant
France
Alexia Roux
alexiaroux.fr
2018

148

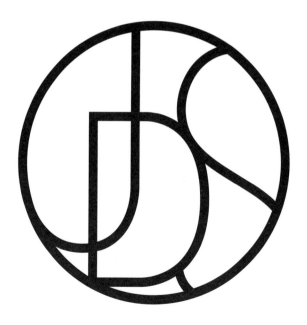

149

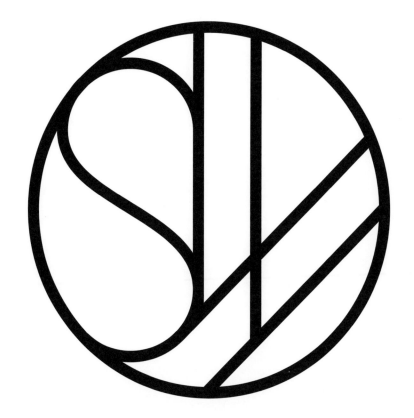

Sweet Whistle
Customisable gifting service
USA
High Tide
hightidenyc.com
2016

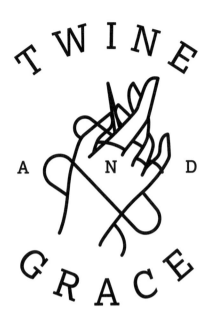

151. Twine & Grace
Handmade gifts
United Kingdom
Angel & Anchor
angelandanchor.com
2017

152. Daily Provisions
Café
USA
Ōyay
oyay.co
2016

153. Izzy's
Restaurant
USA
Ōyay
oyay.co
2014

154. Redhouse
Angus beef farm
USA
Yossi Belkin Design Co.
yossibelkin.com
2017

155. Maryhill Locks
House builder
United Kingdom
Cause & Effect
causeandeffect.design
2018

151

AN ALL DAY AFFAIR
103 EAST 19TH
ST
Daily Provisions
NY
NEW YORK
GATHER & TOAST

152

MIAMI
USA   BEACH
Izzy's
TRMK
- FISH -
AND
OYSTER

153

PREMIUM ANGUS BEEF
+
THE
BAKERSFIELD
CALIFORNIA
RANCH
93314
GRASS FED & FINISHED

154

MARYHILL LOCKS
G 2 0
WHITELAW STREET

155

156. Rinker
Design studio
USA
Rinker Design Co.
rinker.co
2016

157. Grado
High-end headphone
& audio manufacturer
USA
High Tide
hightidenyc.com
2017

EVOLUTION THROUGH EXPLORATION

RINKER
DESIGN Co
VENICE
CA-USA

ESTD 2003

156

HANDBUILT IN BROOKLYN NEW YORK

HEADPHONES
EST
GRADO LABS
1953
CARTRIDGES

THREE GENERATIONS OF SOUND

157

158. Hendrickson General Hardware
General hardware store
USA
Brandon Nickerson
bnicks.com
2017

159. Green Bench Brewing Co
Brewery
USA
Break Maiden
breakmaiden.co
2019

160

161

162

163

164

165

166

167

160. Omar Nieto
Law firm
Spain
Diferente
diferente.info
2016

161. Pollard We Are
Photography
New Zealand
makebardo
makebardo.com
2017

162. Sinclair and Rice
Catering
United Kingdom
Cause & Effect
causeandeffect.design
2018

163. Jädelino
Artisan ice cream shop
Italy/Finland
Kuudes Helsinki
kuudes.com
2017

164. Skin Laundry
Laser-based facial
& skincare line
USA
High Tide
hightidenyc.com
2018

165. The Stand Food Hall
Restaurant
USA
Yossi Belkin Design Co.
yossibelkin.com
2017

166. The Townhouse
Bar & restaurant
Turkey
Studio Born
studioborn.co
2019

167. Regenerative Resorts
Boutique resort booking
International
Brandon Nickerson
bnicks.com
2018

168. Honeysuckle Precinct
Destination
Australia
Shorthand Studio
shorthandstudio.com
2016

169. Apartment
Homewares store
Australia
Mildred & Duck
mildredandduck.com
2018

170. Southern Bureau
Exhibition design
Australia
Mildred & Duck
mildredandduck.com
2018

171. Cale&Cael
Fashion brand
USA
Diferente
diferente.info
2018

172. Priah
Clothing brand
Colombia
Diferente
diferente.info
2018

168

169

170

171

172

173

174

175

176

177

173. Hurley
Surf apparel
Australia
Stuart Smythe
stuartsmythe.com
2016

174. Groce Family Farm
Farm
USA
Misc. Goods Co.
misc-design-co.com
2015

**175. PT'S Coffee
Roasting Co.**
Coffee roasting
USA
Carpenter Collective
carpentercollective.com
2017

**176. Featherbed Coffee
Roasters**
Coffee roaster
United Kingdom
Stuart Smythe
stuartsmythe.com
2018

177. Aroh Co.
Manufacturing & design
USA
Misc. Goods Co.
misc-design-co.com
2016

178. Filidoro
Brewery
Argentina
Tricota Agency
tricota.com.ar
2016

179. Mitte Brot
Artisan bakery
Turkey
Studio Born
studioborn.co
2018

178

179

180. Maitland Pregnancy Massage
Remedial massage
Australia
Shorthand Studio
shorthandstudio.com
2019

181. BetterBreads
Vegan bakery
Singapore
Diferente
diferente.info
2018

180

181

182. Jorvik House
Boutique hotel
United Kingdom
Fettle
fettledesign.com
2018

183. Kokekaffe
Coffee roastery
Taiwan, China
2TIGERS Design Studio
2tigersdesign.com
2017

182

183

184

185

184. Num Pang Kitchen
Fast casual food concept
USA
High Tide
hightidenyc.com
2017

185. Adamo
Hammocks & other
accessories for children
Hungary
Classmate Studio
classmatestudio.com
2018

186. Porter Panthers
Volleyball
USA
Brandon Nickerson
bnicks.com
2017

187. Everest
Food
Brazil
Pedro Paulino
pedropaulino.com
2016

188. Little Pines
Early childhood education
& care
Australia
Shorthand Studio
shorthandstudio.com
2016

186

187

188

189. Manufaktura Pierogów
Frozen Polish dumplings
Poland
Dmowski & Co.
dmowski.co
2016

190. Brew Your Mind
Brewery
Hungary
Classmate Studio
classmatestudio.com
2018

189

190

191. Pantai
Tai restaurant
Poland
Dmowski & Co.
dmowski.co
2015

192. Openhaus
Design & concept store
Turkey
Studio Born
studioborn.co
2018

193. Cafetoria
Organic coffee roaster
Finland
Diferente
diferente.info
2018

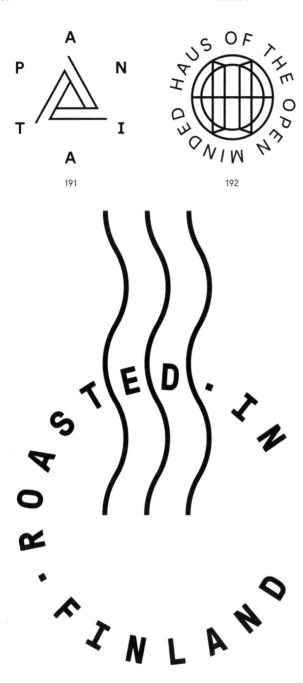

191

192

193

194. Eight Pineapples
Handmade candles
Australia
Tom Broadhurst
tombroadhurstdesign.com
2013

195. Sandro
Fashion
France
Lapetitegrosse/Jeffpag
lapetitegrosse.com
jeffpag.com
1984

194

195

196. Element Skate Company
Apparel, skateboards & accesories
USA
Stuart Smythe
stuartsmythe.com
2016

197. CLVL Apparel Co.
Apparel
New Zealand
Stuart Smythe
stuartsmythe.com
2014

198   199

200

201   202

198. Modern Citizen
Apparel
United Kingdom
Alan Cheetham
behance.net/booyah
2015

199. VELAS
Event venue
Mexico
Communal
communal.mx
2016

200. The Changer
Beverage/mulled wine syrup
New Zealand
makebardo
makebardo.com
2017

201. Chicago Sign Co
Sign painting
USA
Break Maiden
breakmaiden.co
2018

202. Bookitlist
Adventure & travel company
United Kingdom
Alan Cheetham
behance.net/booyah
2016

NO BAD DAYS

203. No Bad Days
Notebook
France
Alexia Roux
alexiaroux.fr
2018

CRAFTS FROM

JOHN STOGAN

MADE *In the* USA

ENDULGE IN THE
FRUIT OF YOUR LABOR

204. John Stogan
Arts & crafts
USA
Brandon Nickerson
bnicks.com
2016

◆

HOUSE
OF
VOLTAIRE

ᴜᴘꜱᴛᴀɪᴿˢ ᴀᵀ

◆

19 BRUTON PLACE W1
LONDON

◆

205. House of Voltaire
Pop-up shop
United Kingdom
A Practice for Everyday Life
apracticeforeverydaylife.com
2010

206

207

208

209

206. Zombie
Animation
Brazil
Pedro Paulino
pedropaulino.com
2017

207. Letter Alley
Independent coffee shop
& library
Italy
Luminor Sign Co.
luminorsignco.com
2011

208. Folio Society
Publisher
United Kingdom
Luminor Sign Co.
luminorsignco.com
2012

209. Lakehouse
Venture capital firm
USA
High Tide
hightidenyc.com
2019

210. Jonas Granfors
Artisan carpenter
Finland
Werklig
werklig.com
2018

211. Sequoia River Dance
Bed & breakfast
USA
Courier Design Co
courierdesign.com
2017

212. Brick Creative
Video production
Break Maiden
breakmaiden.co
2018

211

212

213. **Fantastic Villa Marzipan**
Entertainment
Switzerland
Jeffpag
jeffpag.com
1991

214. **MiW's Tail a Fairy Tale**
Manufacturing company
Japan
Grand Deluxe
grand-deluxe.com
2016

215. **Jansal Valley**
Specialty foods
USA
Ōyay
oyay.co
2016

216. **Ossipee Distilling**
Distillery
USA
Ōyay
oyay.co
2017

217. **Flora**
Botanical alchemist
USA
Krinsky Design
krinskydesign.com
2017

213

214

215

216

217

218. Hotel Carmel
Hotel
USA
Rinker Design Co.
rinker.co
2016

219. Marohnic, Tomek & Gjoic
Law practice
Croatia
Bunch
bunchdesign.com
2017

220. Luis Guilherme
Personal trainer
Brazil
Pedro Paulino
pedropaulino.com
2019

221. Panakeia Hot Pot
Hot pot restaurant
Taiwan, China
2TIGERS Design Studio
2tigersdesign.com
2017

222. Company 251
Event space/wedding venue
USA
Parker
designbyparker.com
2016

223. Madison Coffee & Tea
Coffee shop
USA
Misc. Goods Co.
misc-design-co.com
2014

219

220

221

222

223

224. Dalton
Winery
Israel
Studio Koniak
koniakdesign.com
2016

225. Drifters Fish
Fishery
USA
Parker
designbyparker.com
2016

226. Buddhafields
Holistic center & hotel
Anagrama
anagrama.com
Mexico
2014

224

225

226

227. The Levee
Hotel
Israel
Studio Koniak
koniakdesign.com
2019

228. Salón Sociedad
Bar
Mexico
Communal
communal.mx
2017

227

228

229. Georges Eugene
Furniture store
France
Alexia Roux
alexiaroux.fr
2018

230   231

232

234   235

230. The Loft Cinema
Art house cinema
USA
Cast Iron Design
castirondesign.com
2012

231. Treadwell
Epoxy flooring
USA
Perky Bros
perkybros.com
2015

232. Valentto
Olivarera Italo-Mexicana's
virgin olive oil brand
Mexico
Anagrama
anagrama.com
2013

233. Otoño Jamón de Huelva
Iberian ham
Spain
Tres Tipos Gráficos
trestiposgraficos.com
2016

234. Jaffa & Co.
Luxury asset law firm
United Kingdom
alt-design.net
2018

235. Fodi
Online grocery store
Sweden
Bunch
bunchdesign.com
2017

236. Alfred
Beer
Belgium
Chilli
chilli.be
2015

237. Hanson
Asset management
Ascend Studio
ascendstudio.co.uk
2019

236

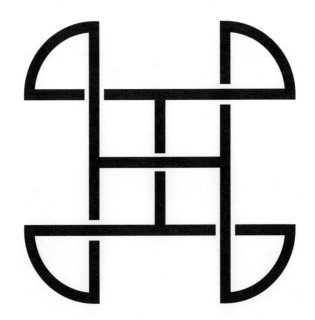

237

238

239

240

241

242

243. Noble Coffee Roasting
Coffee roasting
USA
Carpenter Collective
carpentercollective.com
2019

26. Northern Horse Park
Equestrian center
Japan
6D
6d-k.com
2011

245. Frontier Provisions
Apparel store
South Africa
Courier Design Co
courierdesign.com
2018

246. Pierogi
Polish food
Austria
Bruch—Idee&Form
studiobruch.com
2015

243

244

245

246

247. Brick Creative
Video production
USA
Break Maiden
breakmaiden.co
2018

248. Bistro Georgette
French inspired street food
USA
Break Maiden
breakmaiden.co
2018

249. Tindeco Wharf
Residential
USA
Ashton Design
ashton-design.com
2014

250. Bikes on Wheels
Bicycle sales & service
Canada
Doublenaut
doublenaut.com
2018

251. Liars Bench
Beer Company
Brewery
USA
HAM
madebyham.com
2016

247

248

249

250

251

252. Chicago Sign Co
Sign painting
USA
Break Maiden
breakmaiden.co
2018

253. Ybor City Latin Quater
Self-initiated
USA
Break Maiden
breakmaiden.co
2018

PLATES + POURS

254. The Brass Onion
Restaurant
USA
Carpenter Collective
carpentercollective.com
2018

255

256

257

258

255. Harry's
Men's grooming company
USA
Brandon Nickerson
bnicks.com
2016

256. Penny Post
Retail
USA
SDCO Partners
sdcopartners.com
2017

257. Rotonda No.102
Restaurant
Mexico
Communal
communal.mx
2016

258. Jadelino
Artisan ice cream shop
Italy
Kuudes
kuudes.fi
2017

CRESTS

259. KIPP:DC
Education
USA
Ashton Design
ashton-design.com
2015

260. Odabashian
Hand-woven rugs
USA, Mexico & China
Anagrama
anagrama.com
2016

261. Anthem
Scouting & transfer of
professional football players
from one association football
club to another
2014
Spain, Switzerland & Mexico
Anagrama
anagrama.com
2016

262. Sentry Wealth/Law
Wealth management/law
United Kingdom
Mash Creative
mashcreative.co.uk
2016

263. Pride Homes
Real estate development
USA
Krinsky Design
krinskydesign.com
2017

259

260

261

262

263

264. Stag & Loch
Public house
United Kingdom
Mash Creative
mashcreative.co.uk
2015

265. Van Pur
Polish brewing company
Poland
Mash Creative/Socio Design
mashcreative.co.uk
sociodesign.co.uk
2014

266. Casteels
Real estate
Belgium
Chilli
chilli.be
2019

267. Armento
Hedge fund
Mexico
Communal
communal.mx
2016

268. Potomac Advisors
Financial planning
USA
Krinsky Design
krinskydesign.com
2017

269. Smiths Stables
Horse riding & stables
United Kingdom
Mash Creative
mashcreative.co.uk
2014

270. Independent Leaders
Fashion
United Kingdom
Mash Creative
mashcreative.co.uk
2012

271. Aquila
Music
United Kingdom
Mash Creative
mashcreative.co.uk
2012

264

265

266

267

268

269

270

271

272. Griffin
Self-initiated
USA
Rinker Design Co.
rinker.co
2015

273. Sepsiszentiványi és Kovásznai
Márkus de Deák family coat of arms
Austro-Hungarian
Peltan-Brosz
peltan-brosz.com
2016

274. Century Farms
Real estate/development
USA
Carpenter Collective
carpentercollective.com
2016

275. Tesis
Tea
Mexico
Anagrama
anagrama.com
2016

274

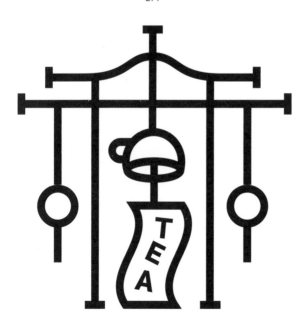

275

276. Baketique
Creative baking
Portugal/South Africa
Brad Cuzen Illustration
& Design
bradcuzen.com
2018

277. The Greater Good
Bar
Canada
Doublenaut
doublenaut.com
2016

276

277

278

279

280

281

282

278. Finkel & Garf
Brewery
USA
Cast Iron Design
castirondesign.com
2014

279. Passport
Cannabis products
Mexico
Saturna Studio
saturnastudio.com
2018

280. La Playa Carmel
Hotel
USA
Rinker Design Co.
rinker.co
2016

281. Judges Court
Boutique hotel
United Kingdom
Fettle
fettledesign.com
2015

282. Rivero González
Wine
Mexico
Anagrama
anagrama.com
2011

283. Circle Crest
Self-initiated
United Kingdom
Aidan Croucher
behance.net/aidancroucher
2018

284. Sunday Suns
Self-initiated
USA
Carpenter Collective
carpentercollective.com
2018

285. Superbowl
Self-initiated
USA
Carpenter Collective
carpentercollective.com
2019

286. Tucana Coffee
Coffee
Canada
Doublenaut
doublenaut.com
2015

287. Three Little Words
Nonprofit
USA
Doublenaut
doublenaut.com
2018

283

284

285

286

287

288. Cluster & Bosk
Film production
Mexico
Communal
communal.mx
2019

289. Sunday Suns
Self-initiated
USA
Carpenter Collective
carpentercollective.com
2019

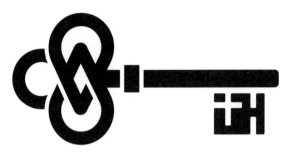

290

290. Thompson Heritage Consultancy
Heritage consultancy
United Kingdom
Fettle
fettledesign.com
2017

291. DeArmond Homebuilders
Home construction company
USA
Austin McKinney
axmckinney.com
2018

292. La Forchetta
Restaurant
Italy
BRVND
brvnd.com
2017

ESTD   1998

DeArmond
HOMEBUILDERS
VERSAILLES, KY

291

est. 1997

la Forchetta

292

293. Amass & G
Interior design
Mexico
Saturna Studio
saturnastudio.com
2015

294. Sofia
Building designed by
architect Cesar Pelli for One
Development Group
Mexico
Anagrama
anagrama.com
2012

293

294

295. Chicago Comb Co
Combs
USA
Courier Design Co
courierdesign.com
2017

296

ANDREW

PINCKNEY

INN

297

298

299

300. Leutellier Tesson Couture
Fashion house
France
Atelier Atlantique
atelieratlantique.fr
2002

FLAGS & RIBBONS

301. Sunday Suns
Self-initiated
USA
Carpenter Collective
carpentercollective.com
2018

302. Stay Salty
Lifestyle brand
Australia
Shorthand Studio
shorthandstudio.com
2015

301

302

303. Southern Most
Apparel
USA
Break Maiden
breakmaiden.co
2017

304. Toothland
Dental services
USA
Type08
type08.com
2019

305. Music City Nashville
Golf events
USA
Type08
type08.com
2019

306. Milk Jagger Café
Coffee house
Russla
Dmitry Neal
dmitryneal.ru
2017

307. Premio Lorenzo Zambrano
Excellence award
Mexico
Communal
communal.mx
2017

308. SKR
Association for the
development of Koszalin city
Poland
Mateusz Turbinski
turbinski.com
2015

309. Lukács László Vienna
Fashion
Austria
Peltan-Brosz
peltan-brosz.com
2014

310. Limans
Luxury real estate
Mexico
Saturna Studio
saturnastudio.com
2017

308

309

310

311. Common Wealth
Finance
USA
Austin McKinney
axmckinney.com
2018

312. The Athletic Ink
Sports editorial
USA
Rinker Design Co.
rinker.co
2017

313. Baked
Artisanal bakery & café
USA
Hinterland
hinterlandstudio.com
2018

314. Hollywood Tower Hotel
Self-initiated
USA
Austin McKinney
axmckinney.com
2017

311   312

313

314

315. Permanent Records
Tattoo gallery
USA
Titus Smith & Seth Gale
permanent-records.co
2016

316. Urbant
Real-estate developer
Mexico
Communal
communal.mx
2016

317. Papiery Wartościowe
Stationery shop
Poland
Dmowski & Co.
dmowski.co
2016

318. Exempt from Theory
School ranking system
Poland
Edgar Bąk Studio
edgarbak.info
2018

319. North Capital
Hedge fund
Mexico
Communal
communal.mx
2016

315

316

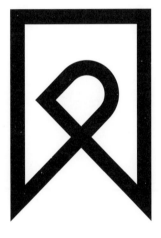

317

318

319

RW

1 7　　6 7

PUE

MEX

IGLESIA
DE
SAN FRANCISCO

320. Lavaderos
Bar
Mexico
Anagrama
anagrama.com
2017

LAURELS

321. Tia Lola
Bakery
Mexico
Anagrama
anagrama.com
2009

322. Brynäs IF
Ice hockey team
Swedan
Kurppa Hosk
kurppahosk.com
2017

333. Senn Bierwerks
Brewery
USA
Carpenter Collective
carpentercollective.com
2015

334. Boulevard Brewing Co.
Beer
USA
Carpenter Collective
carpentercollective.com
2016

333

334

335. Yoli Tortilleria
Tortilla company
USA
Carpenter Collective
carpentercollective.com
2019

336. Century Farms
Real estate/development
USA
Carpenter Collective
carpentercollective.com
2016

335

336

337

338

339

340

337. MPLS Parks
Non-profit fundraiser
to protect city parks
USA
Leslie Olson
leslielynneolson.com
2017

338. Monte Xanic
Winery
Mexico
Anagrama
anagrama.com
2015

339. All Moringa
Moringa products
USA
Saturna Studio
saturnastudio.com
2016

340. Fuego Brew Co.
Brewery
Costa Rica
Rinker Design Co.
rinker.co
2015

341. Harvest Barbershop
Barbershop
Canada
Doublenaut
doublenaut.com
2018

341

342. Brewing District
Brewing/beer production
USA
Type08
type08.com
2017

343. The Scott
Resort & spa
USA
Rinker Design Co.
rinker.co
2017

342

343

344. Bar Laurel
Restaurant
Canada
Doublenaut
doublenaut.com
2016

345. Ambassade des Arts
Premium tourism
France
Lapetitegrosse/Jeffpag
lapetitegrosse.com
jeffpag.com
2015

346. Café la Nacional
Coffee shop and roaster
Mexico
Anagrama
anagrama.com
2017

347. Lavaderos
Bar
Mexico
Anagrama
anagrama.com
2017

AMBASSADE DES ARTS

Made in secrets

345

CAFÉ LA NACIONAL

Café mexicano de altura

NUM.   66220   MTY.

346

347

Modern Heraldry: Volume 2
Seals, Stamps, Crests & Shields

Edited and produced by Counter-Print.

Design: Jon Dowling & Céline Leterme
Typefaces: Druk and Moderat
Printing and Binding: 1010 Printing International Limited

Publishing: Counter-Print
counter-print.co.uk

First published in the United Kingdom in 2020 by Counter-Print.
©Counter-Print

ISBN: 978-1-9161261-3-8

British Library cataloguing-in-publication data: A catalogue
of this book can be found in the British Library.

With special thanks to all the contributors for their support, time and talent.